How to Draw Manga Clothing Folds Tutorial
Learn to Draw Clothing Folds

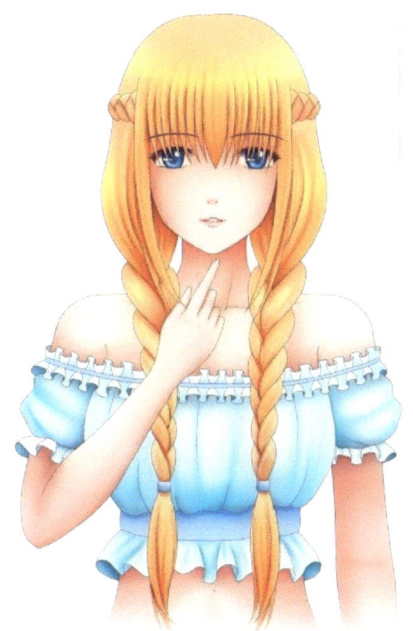

Learn to Draw Series

William T. Dela Peña Jr.

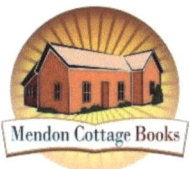

Mendon Cottage Books
JD-Biz Publishing
Download Free Books!

http://MendonCottageBooks.com

Our books are available at

1. Amazon.com
2. Barnes and Noble
3. Itunes
4. Kobo
5. Smashwords
6. Google Play Books

Download Free Books!

http://MendonCottageBooks.com

Table of Contents

INTRODUCTION

Do you find whenever you draw clothing folds it seems not right and not natural? Are you struggling to get your folds to look dynamic? Well, in that case, this book will be your stepping stone to overcome it.

In this book, you will learn how to draw clothing folds in every type of clothing. This book has a lot of illustrations and examples on how to draw folds in a correct way. So relax and learn.

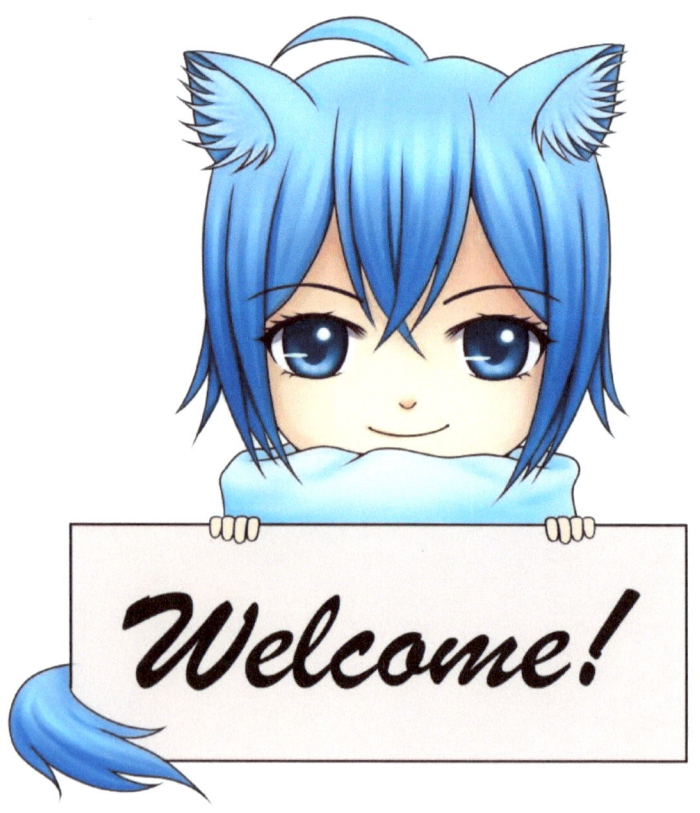

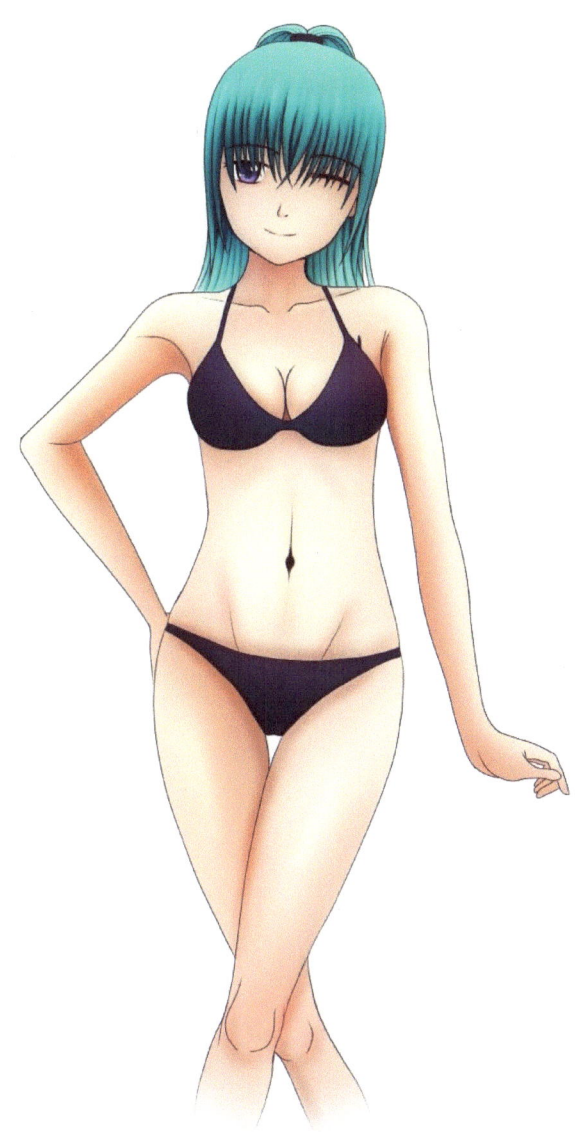

CLOTHING FOLDS TUTORIAL

First, draw your character undressed don't think about the folds of the clothing yet and focus on the form and details of your character. When you're done you can now draw the clothing.

Common mistakes many beginners make when drawing clothing:

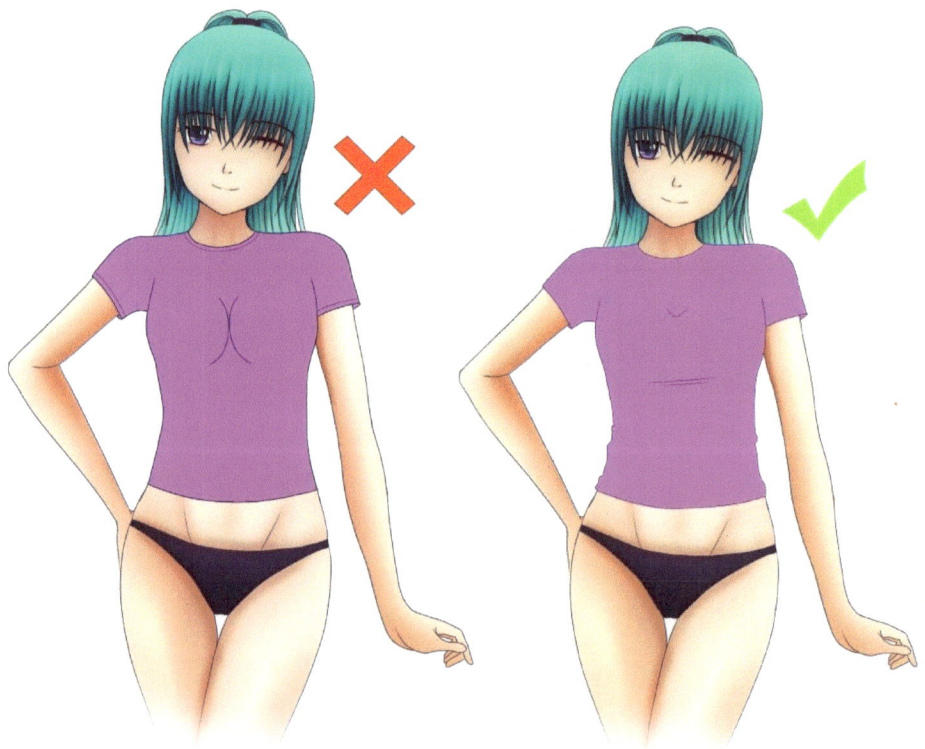

Cleavage doesn't make creases in clothes and keep in mind not to draw it on a regular line in the waistline as shown in the picture to the left. Instead, create some humps on the edge of the clothing as shown in the picture to the right.

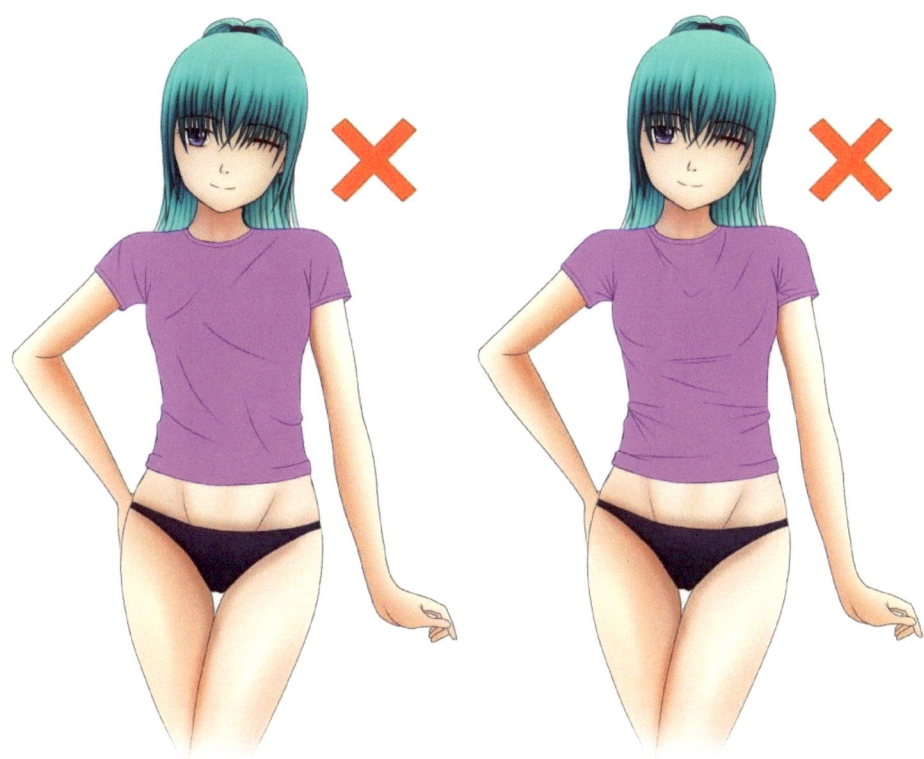

Whenever I look at drawings, drawn by a person who doesn't have the knowledge to draw correct clothing folds, one of the biggest issues is they over draw the lines making up the folds.

The picture to the left shows random lines that make no sense and have no connection with the body contour and the picture to the right shows unnecessary lines that you should avoid doing when drawing.

THE BASIC IDEA OF CLOTHING FOLDS (COMPRESS AND STRETCH)

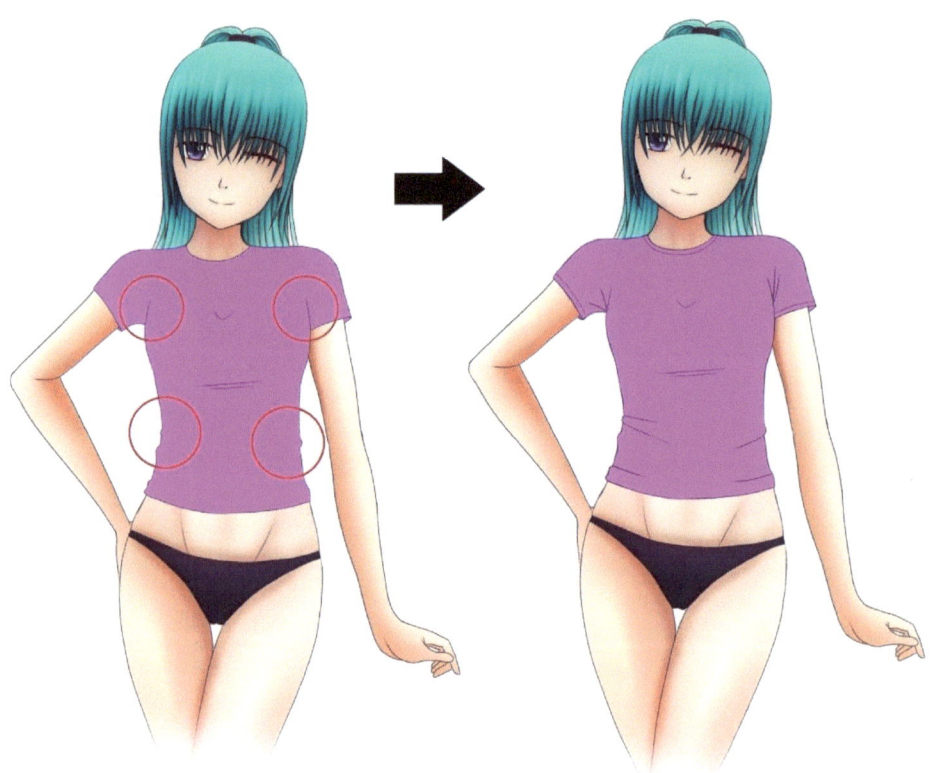

COMPRESSED

Most of the folds are created by compression of the fabrics in certain parts. The encircled areas in the picture above are the areas where you should put the details of the folds.

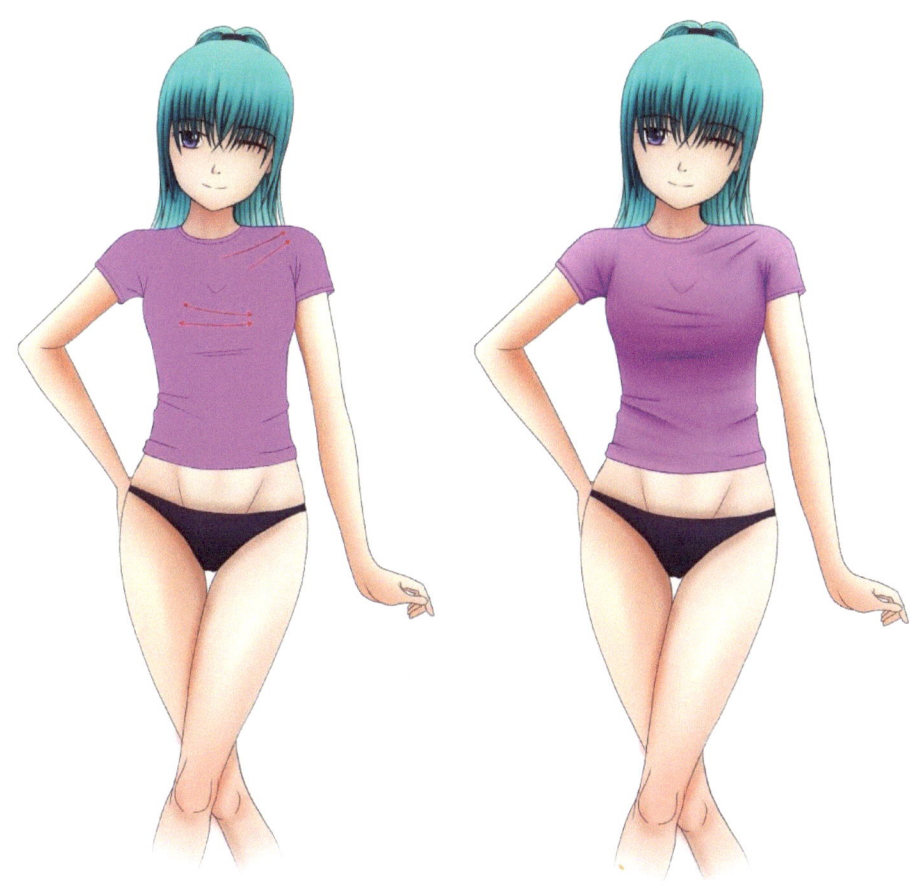

STRETCHED

When there is a tension in a certain area, the fabric is stretched and as a result, it causes folds to the clothing. The picture shows an example of folds created by stretching the fabric.

HOW TO DRAW FOLDS IN SHORTS

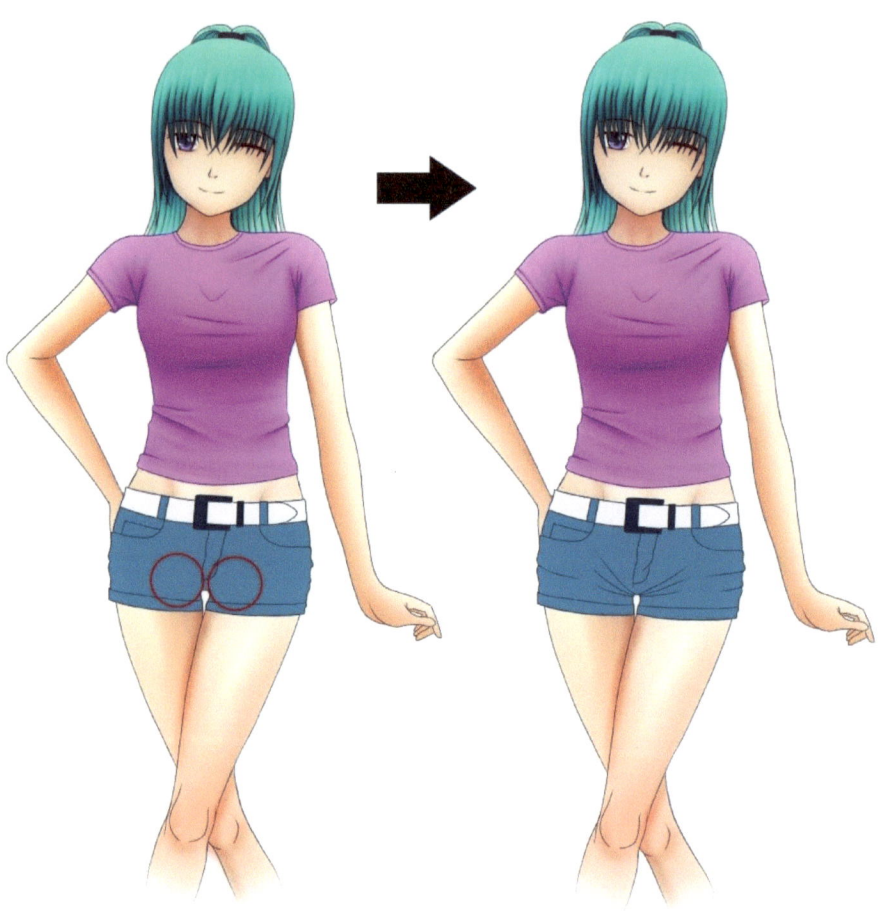

Most of the folds in shorts occur in the crotch area as shown by the picture to the left indicated by the encircled part. The folds are created by a compression.

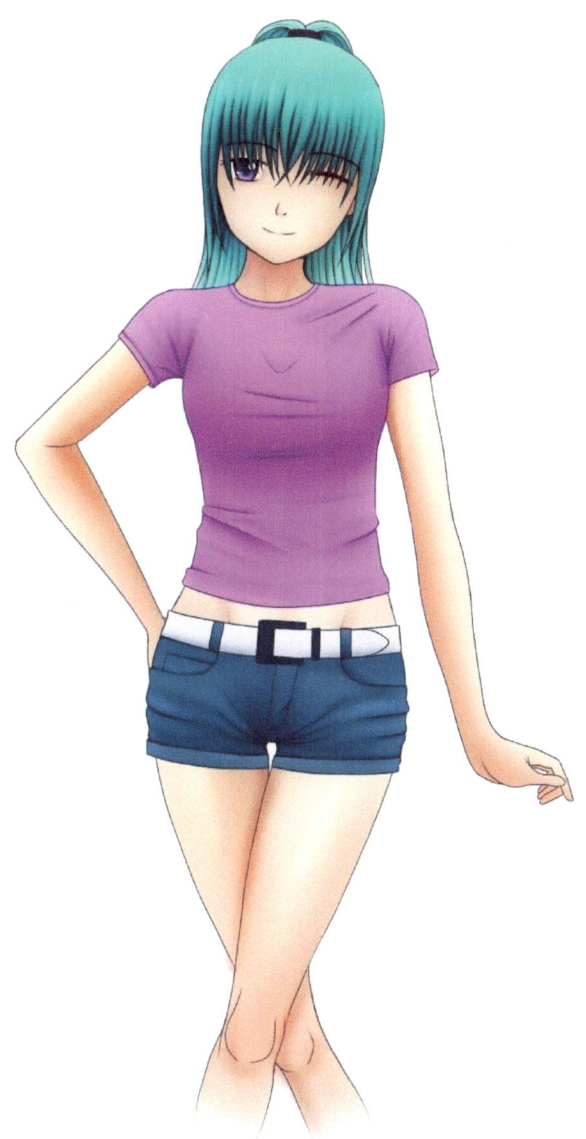

Then add some shading, keep in mind to make a darker shade to the crotch area because light falls minimally on this part of the shorts.

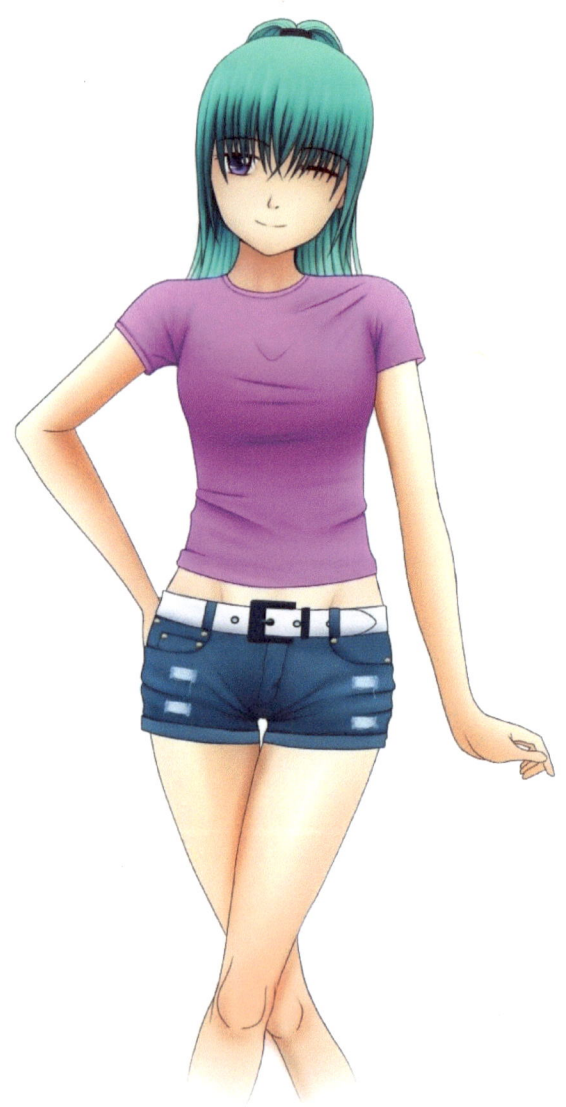

Finally add the finishing touches. Put some holes in the belt and some rivets to the short as shown in the picture to make it metallic use the layer effects in Photoshop called bevel and emboss. Then I also stylized the short by adding some shredded areas.

DRAWING FOLDS IN THICK FABRIC

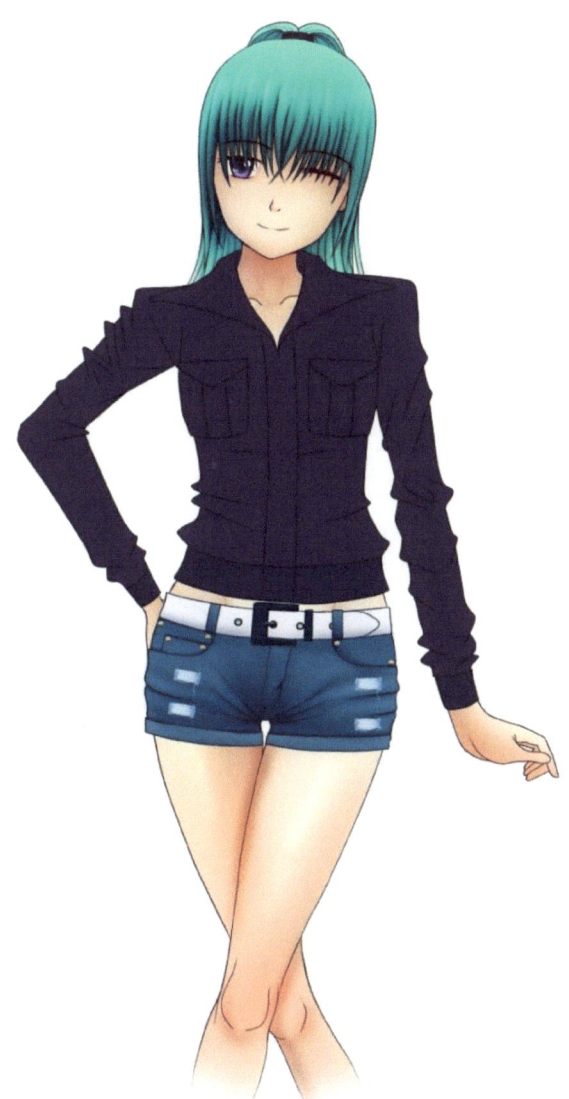

The shape of the folds also varies from the type of fabric the item was made with. Thick materials create sharp edges, for example, the leather jacket that the character is wearing above.

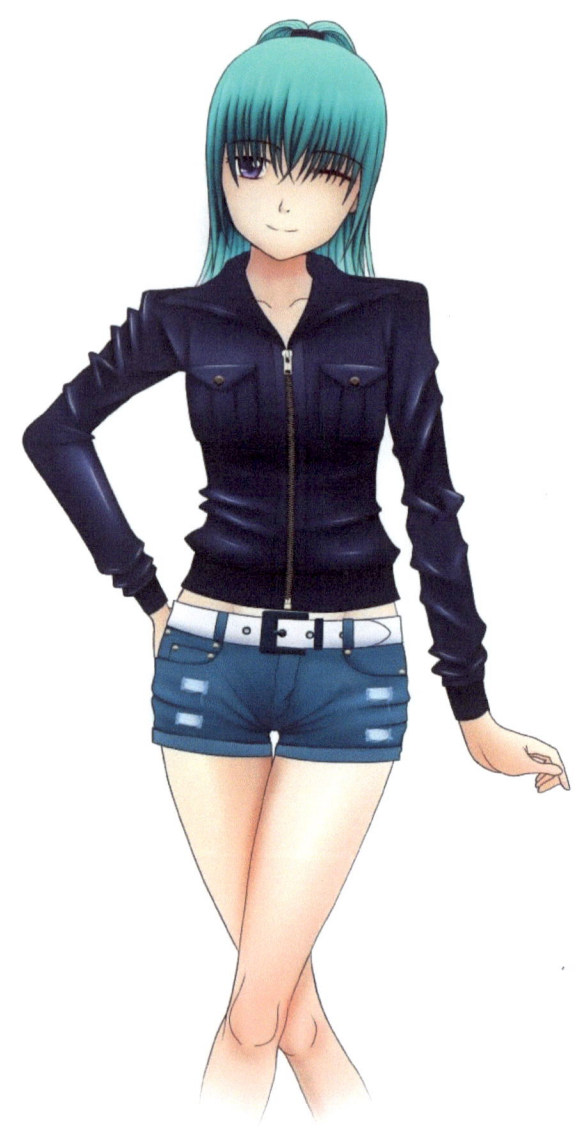

Also keep in mind that materials like leather attract more light so make it shiny and make some minimal white highlighting, as shown in the picture above.

HOW TO DRAW SKIRTS

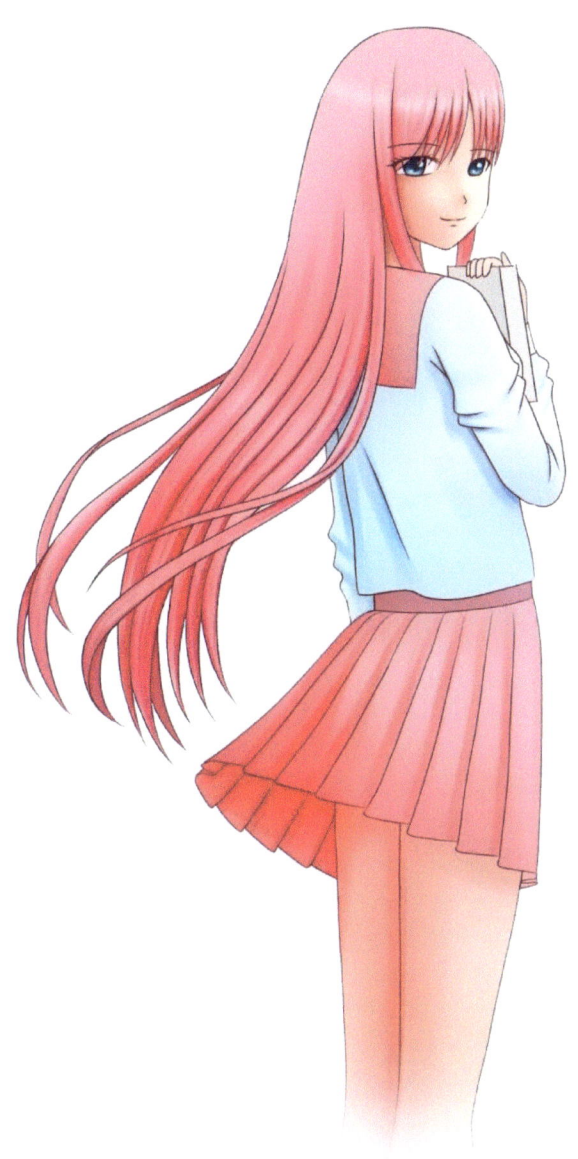

HOW TO DRAW SKIRTS

When drawing the skirt pay attention to the volume. The volume must be consistent when the skirt is flipped away at the back. See the picture below.

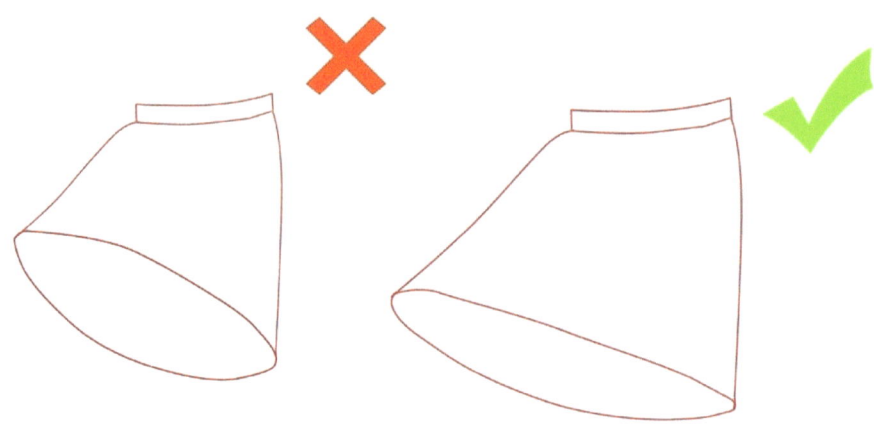

So now let's draw a typical school uniform skirt, first draw the skirt in basic structure like the picture below then draw lightly the oval below the biggest hole in the skirt as shown in the picture below.

Step: 1

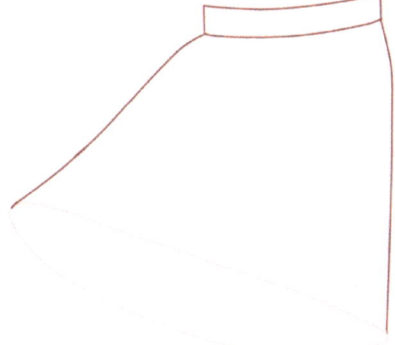

Then draw a series of lines below the waistline of the skirt making the line go slightly over the oval.

Step: 2

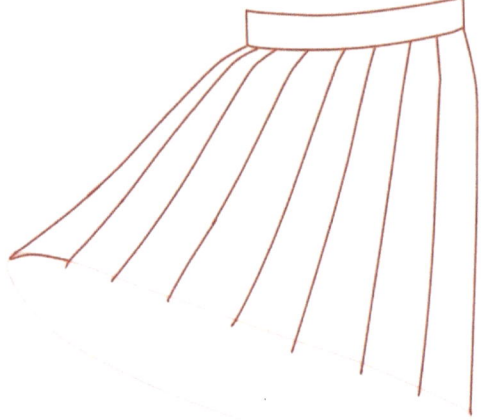

Then make a connection from the slanting line to the oval and as a result, it will create a serrated pattern.

Step: 3

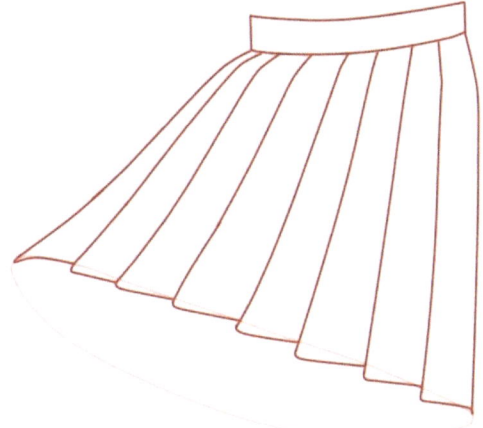

Then do it on the opposite side, keep in mind you will need to draw the serrated pattern of the skirt in the opposite direction of the first pattern.

Step: 4

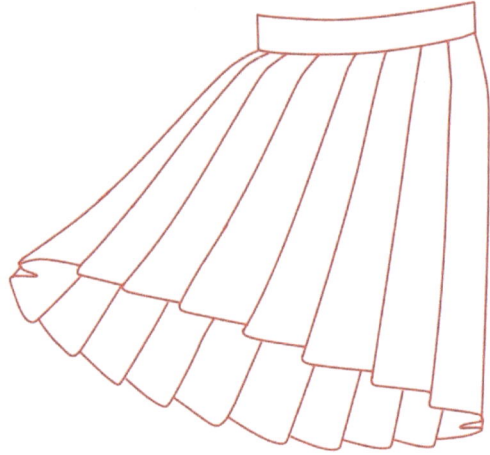

DRAWING FOLDS IN PANTS (JEANS)

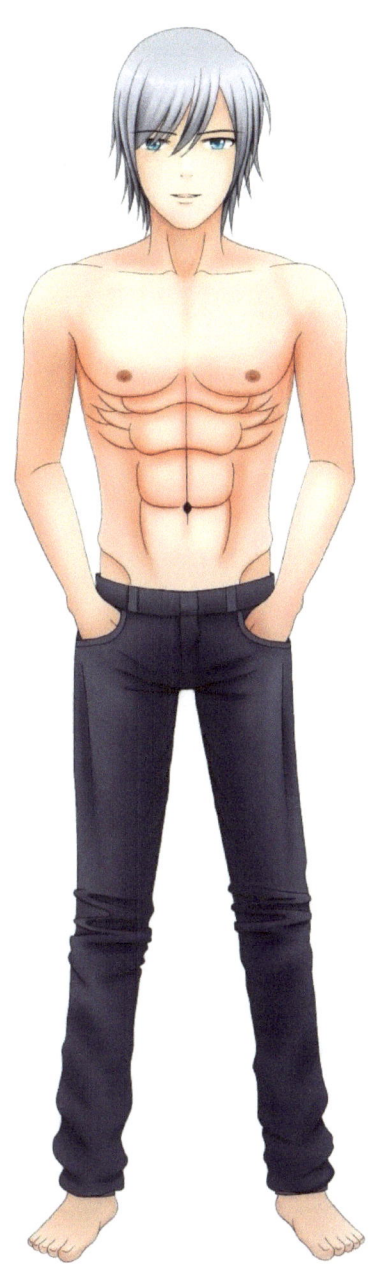

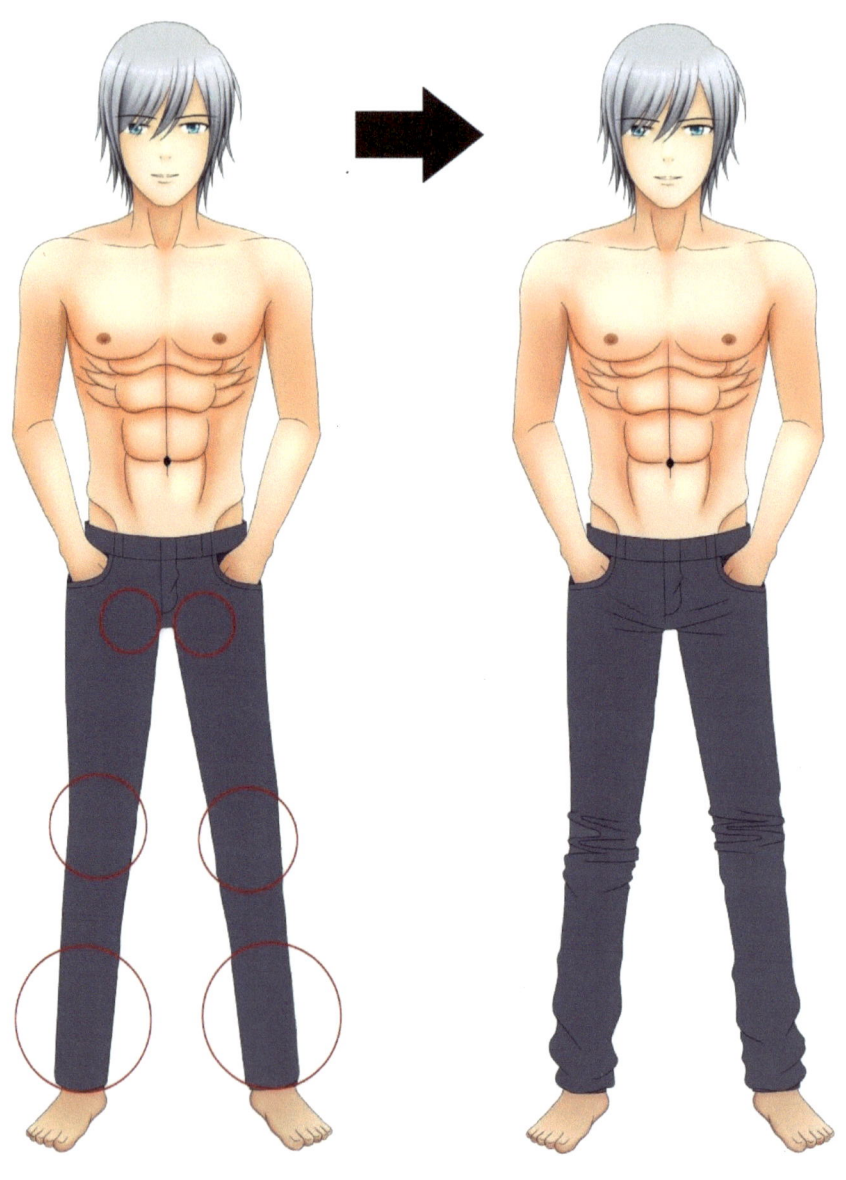

The encircled areas are the areas where the details of the folds will be, they are mainly compressed folds. Also keep in mind you will need to draw a zigzag pattern at area of the knee as shown in the picture.

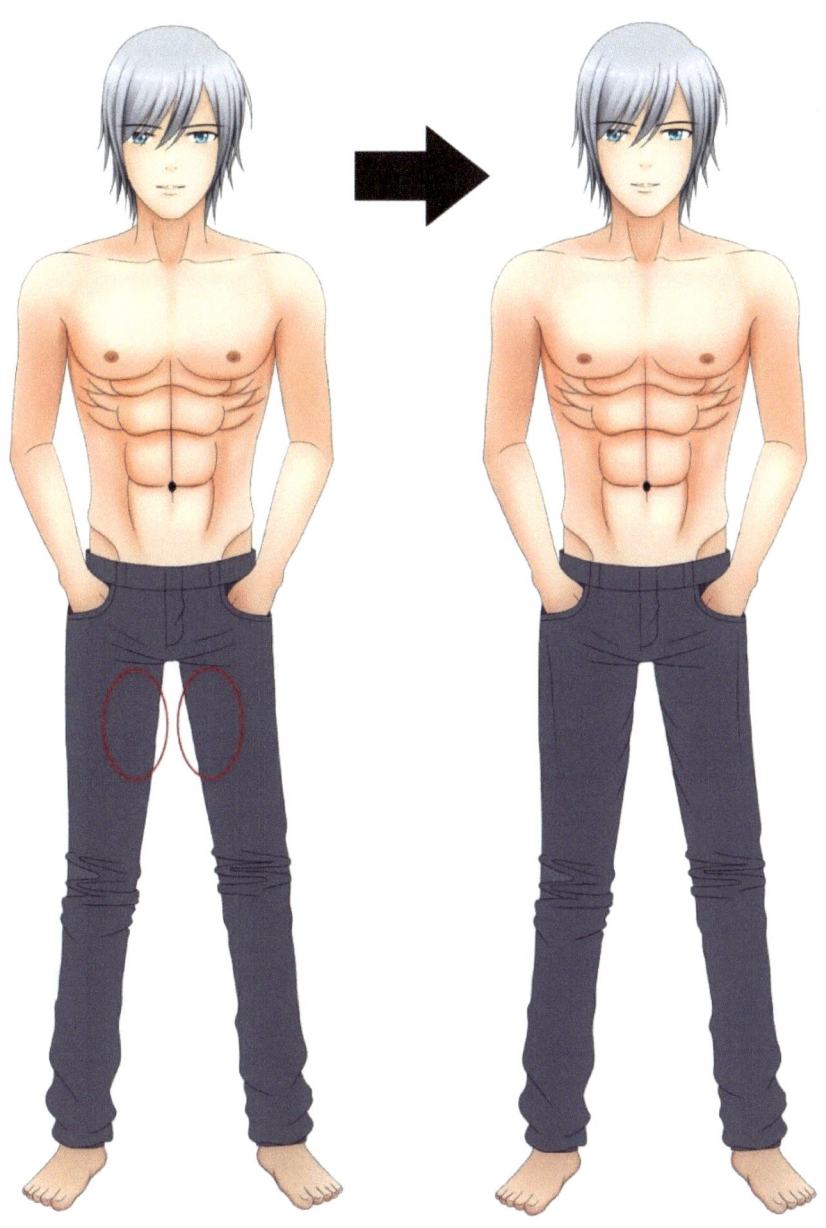

The encircled areas are the areas of a tension, draw parallel lines to give an illusion of stretched areas in the pants.

DRAWING FOLDS IN FORMAL ATTIRE

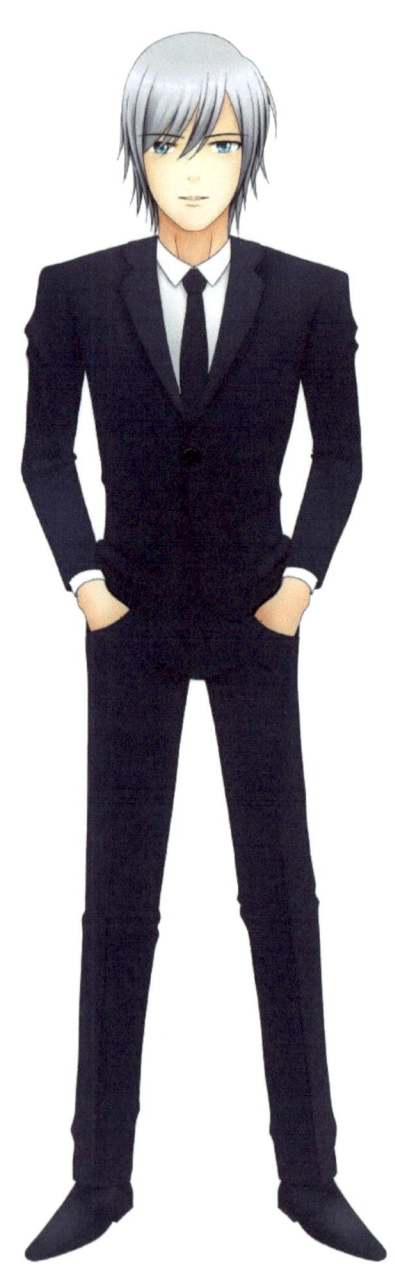

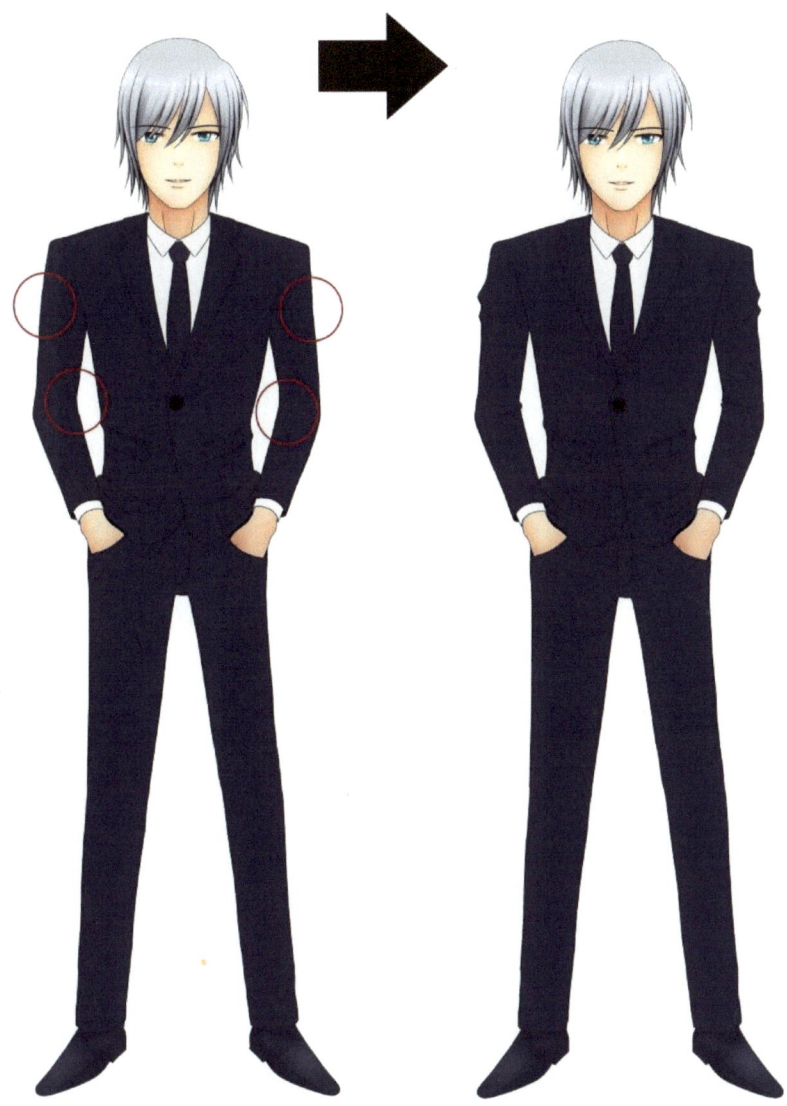

When drawing the coat keep in mind to make the upper portion edge of the shoulder angular as shown in the picture and make only minimal folds. The encircled areas are the areas where one needs to put the details of the folds.

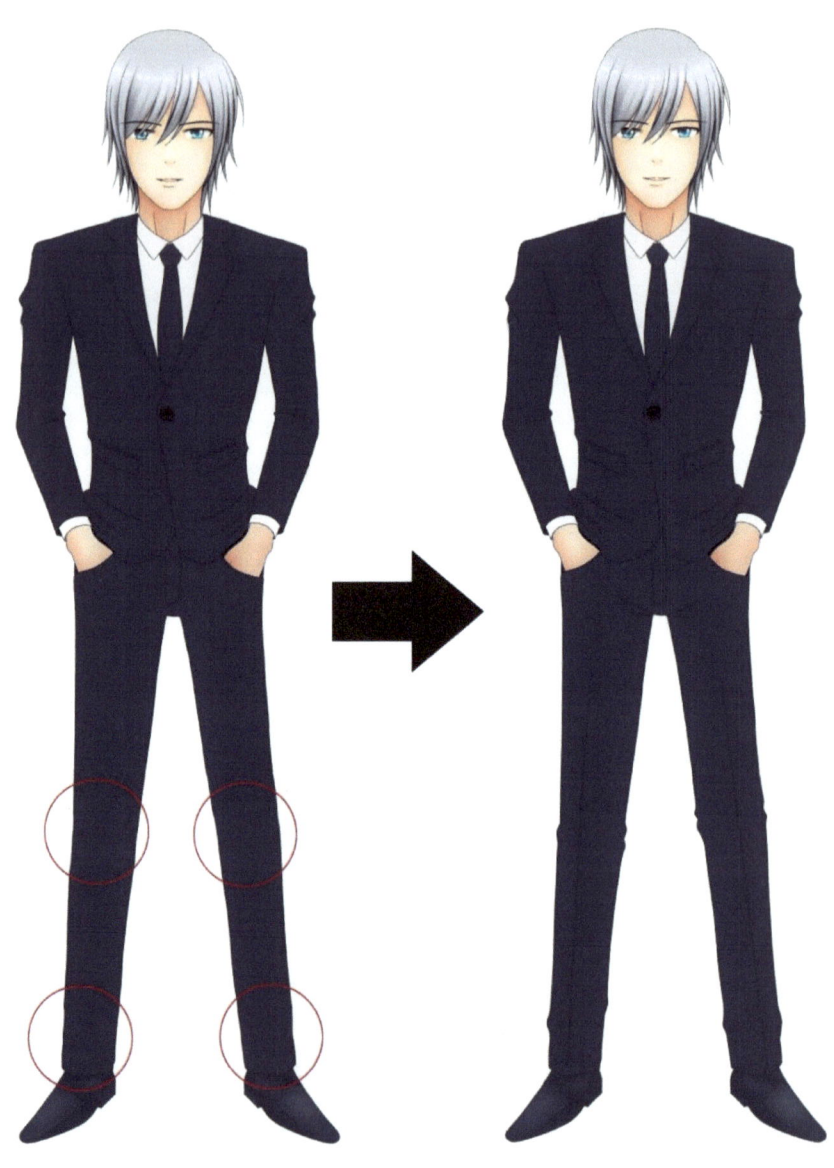

Also in the part of the pants make the folds minimal. In my case I only put some humps on the edge of the pants and don't forget to draw a straight line at the center of the leg area.

HOW TO DRAW FRILLS

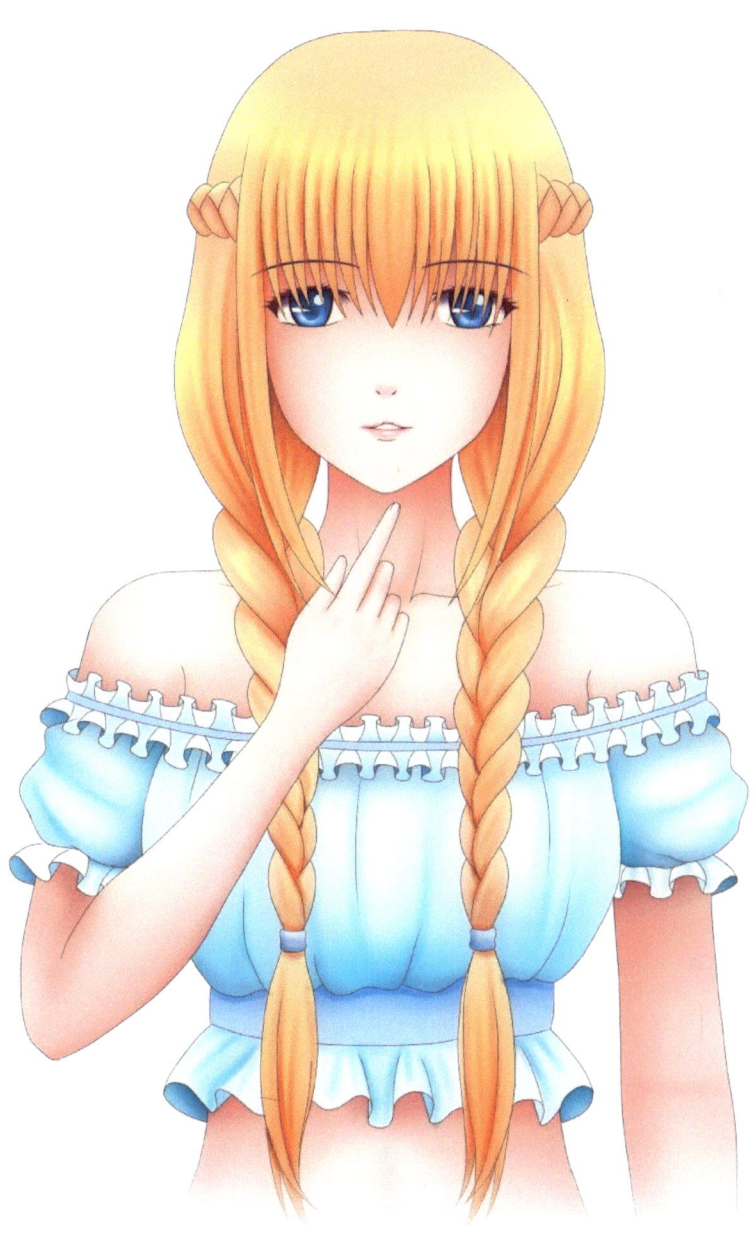

First draw a line pattern like the picture below, keep the shape of the pattern randomize so that it will look natural. Also keep in mind; you will need to make the shape of the pattern slightly angular below.

Step: 1

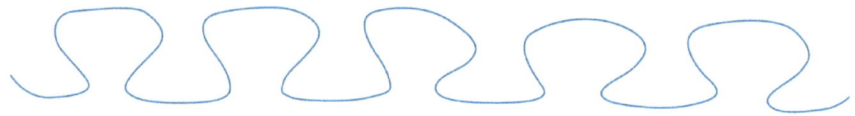

Then draw a slanting line that connects to the top of the line pattern, as shown in the picture below.

Step: 2

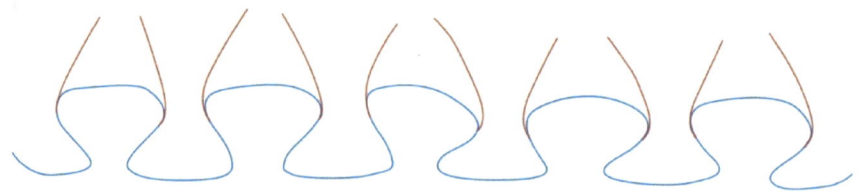

Finally, draw a straight line inside the pattern and make an enclosed path as shown in the picture below.

Step: 3

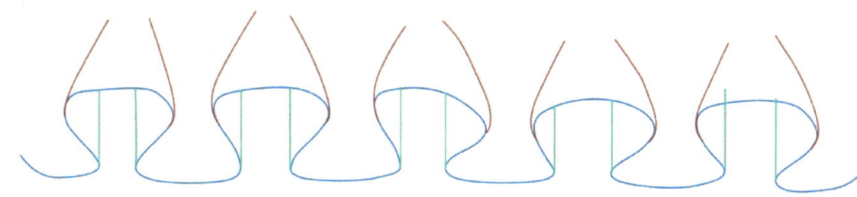

Be sure you make a darker shade on the enclosed path when coloring, to make an illusion of depth as shown in the picture below

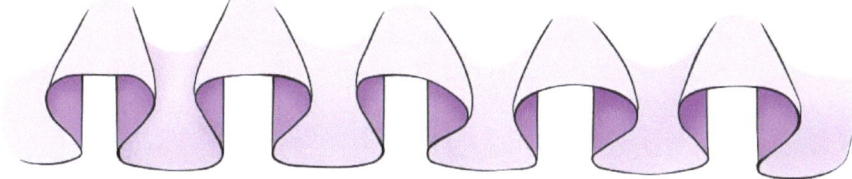

Frills can be also made from flowing curves that has no pattern like the picture below.

Step: 1

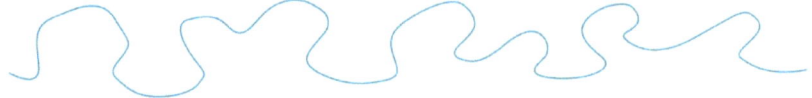

Then draw a line at edge of every curve as shown in the picture below

Step: 2

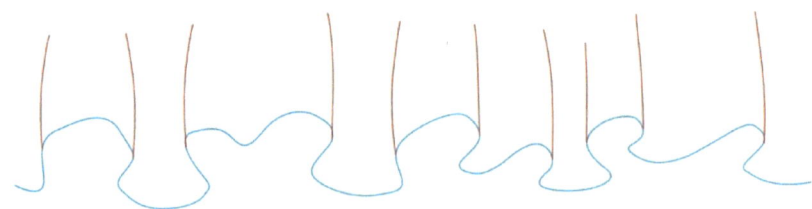

Then lastly, draw a straight line inside the pattern and make an enclosed path as shown in the picture below.

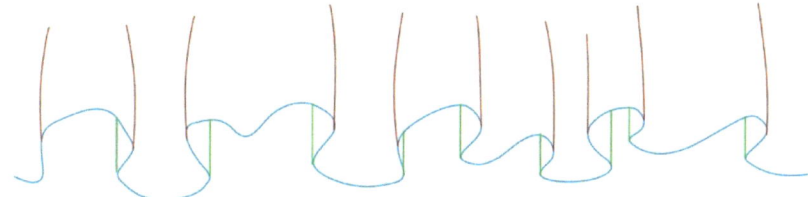

Again, remember to make the enclosed path darker, it helps create the illusion of depth.

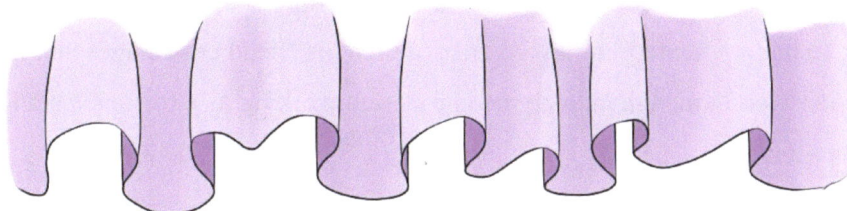

Author Bio

William T. Dela Peña Jr.

William T. Dela Pena Jr. was born in Tondo, Manila but he grew up in their province in Delfin Albano, Isabela. When he was a child his parents and his relatives always get mad at him, because of his unusual behavior, he is hyperactive and filled with curiosity around his surroundings. He always draws what he sees and what he thinks and from there he discovered his passion for arts. During his school years, he earned a lot of awards in art competitions.

He took BS in Information technology, but unfortunately, he was not able to finish his course due to some reasons. Then he decided to go back to Manila and to work as a graphic artist. While he was working as a graphic artist, he spends his free time in drawing anime then his friends that are Otakus notice that he has a potential in drawing manga then his friend encourages him to get involved in manga industry and he started working as a freelance manga illustrator.

Check out some of the other JD-Biz Publishing books

Gardening Series on Amazon

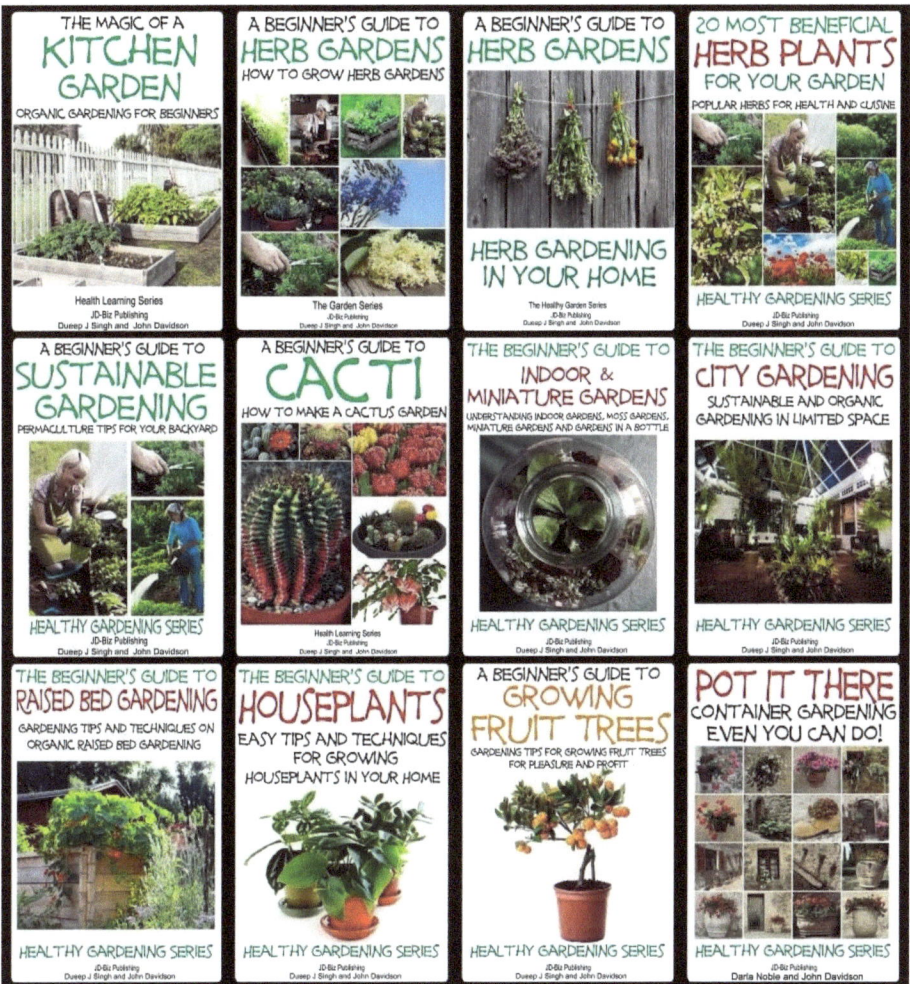

Download Free Books!

http://MendonCottageBooks.com

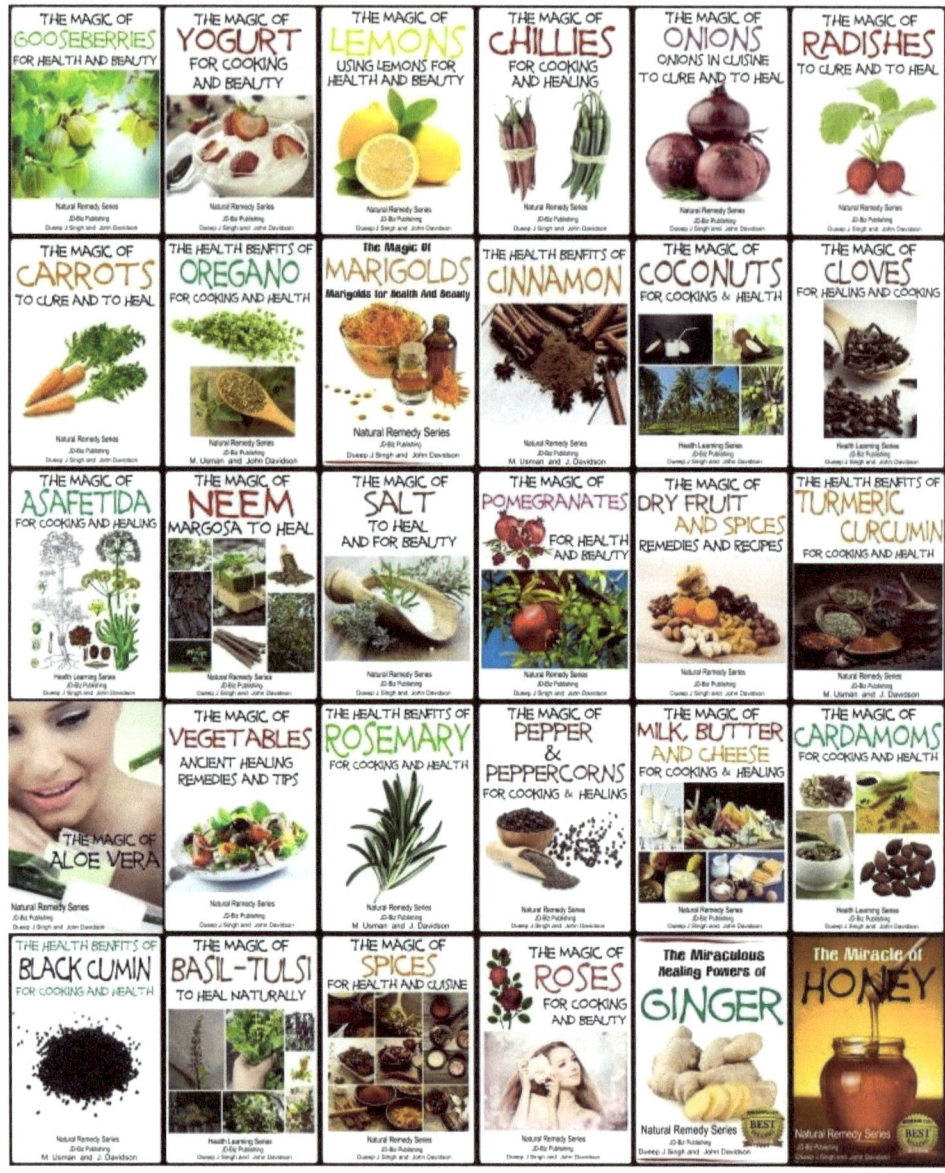

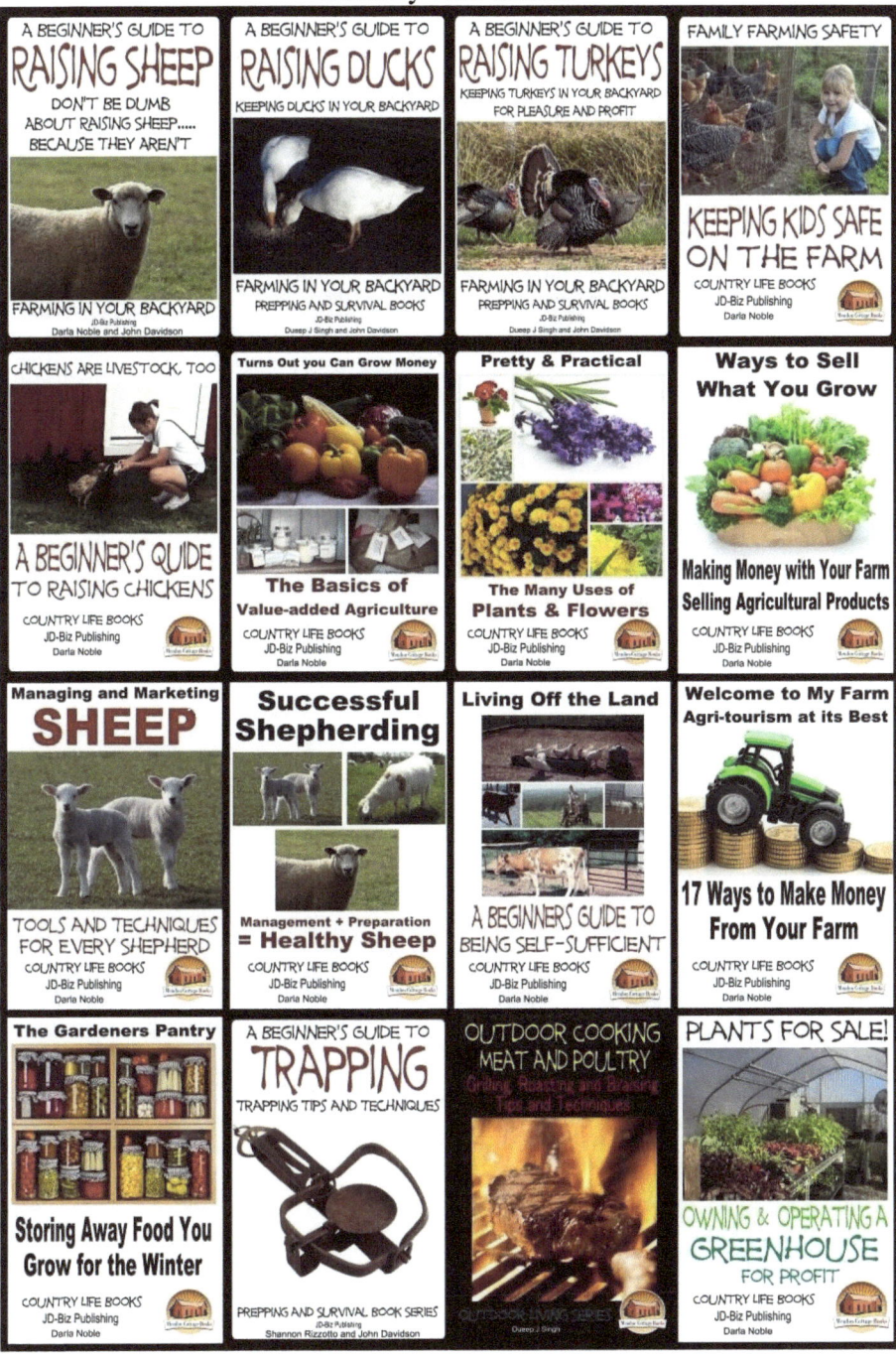

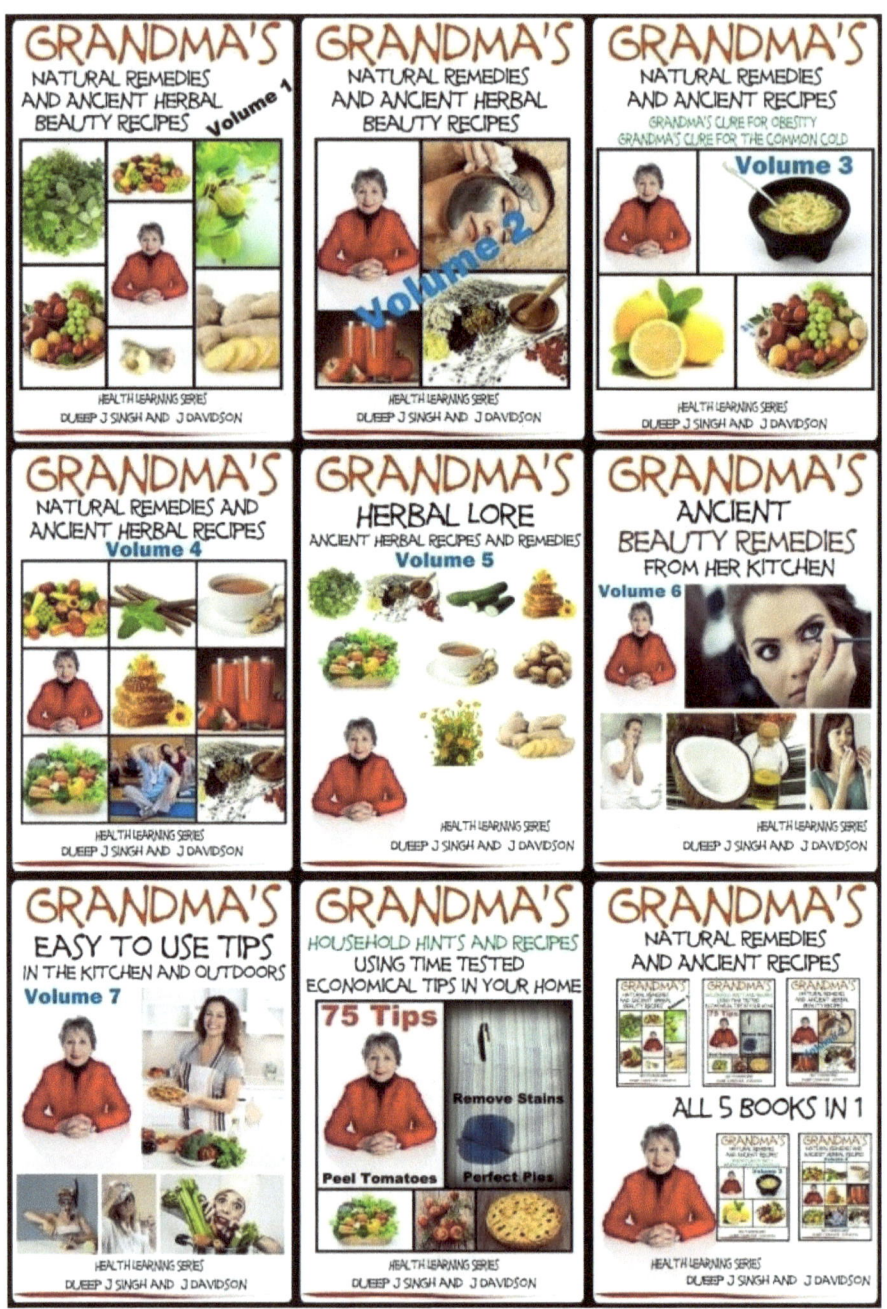

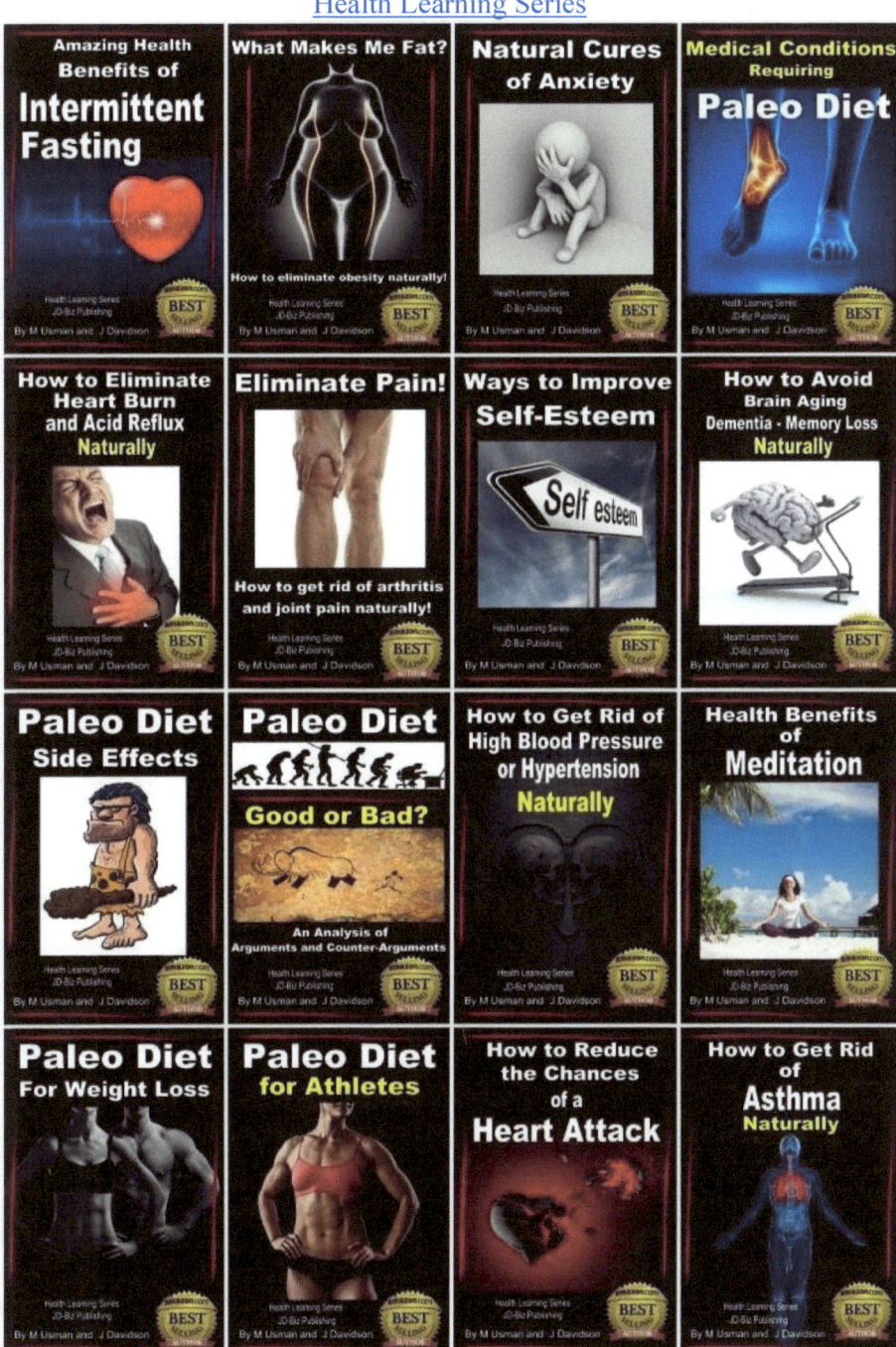

Amazing Animal Book Series

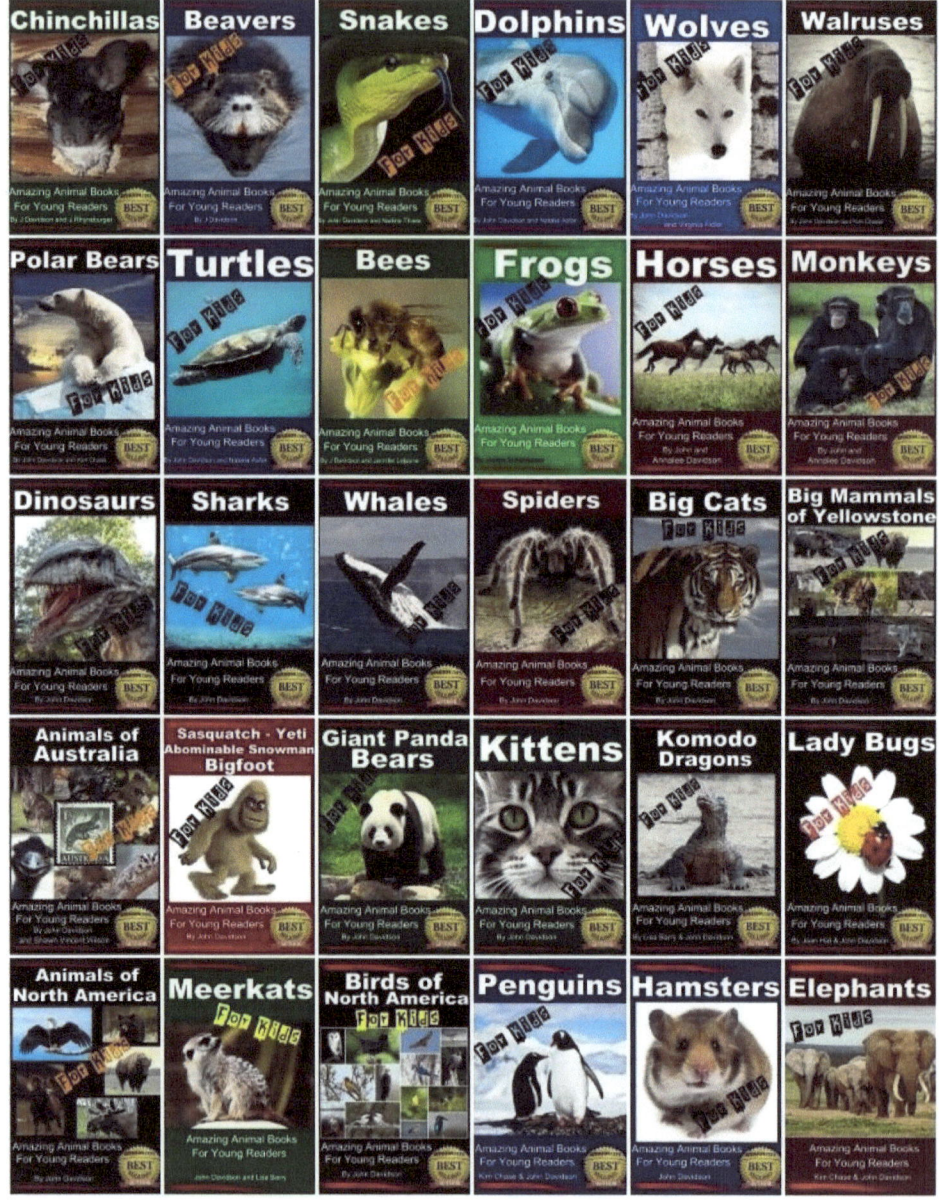

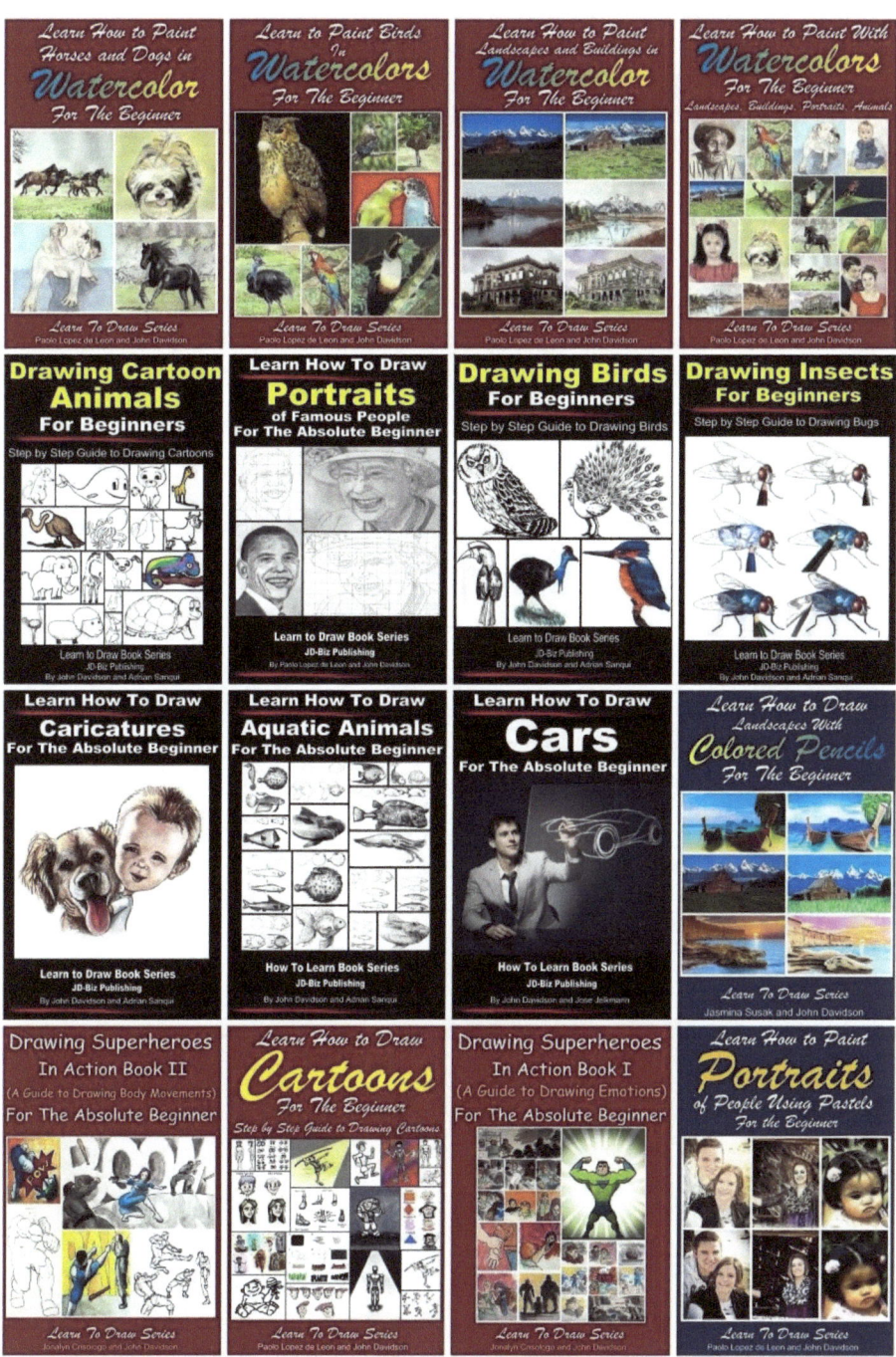

How to Build and Plan Books

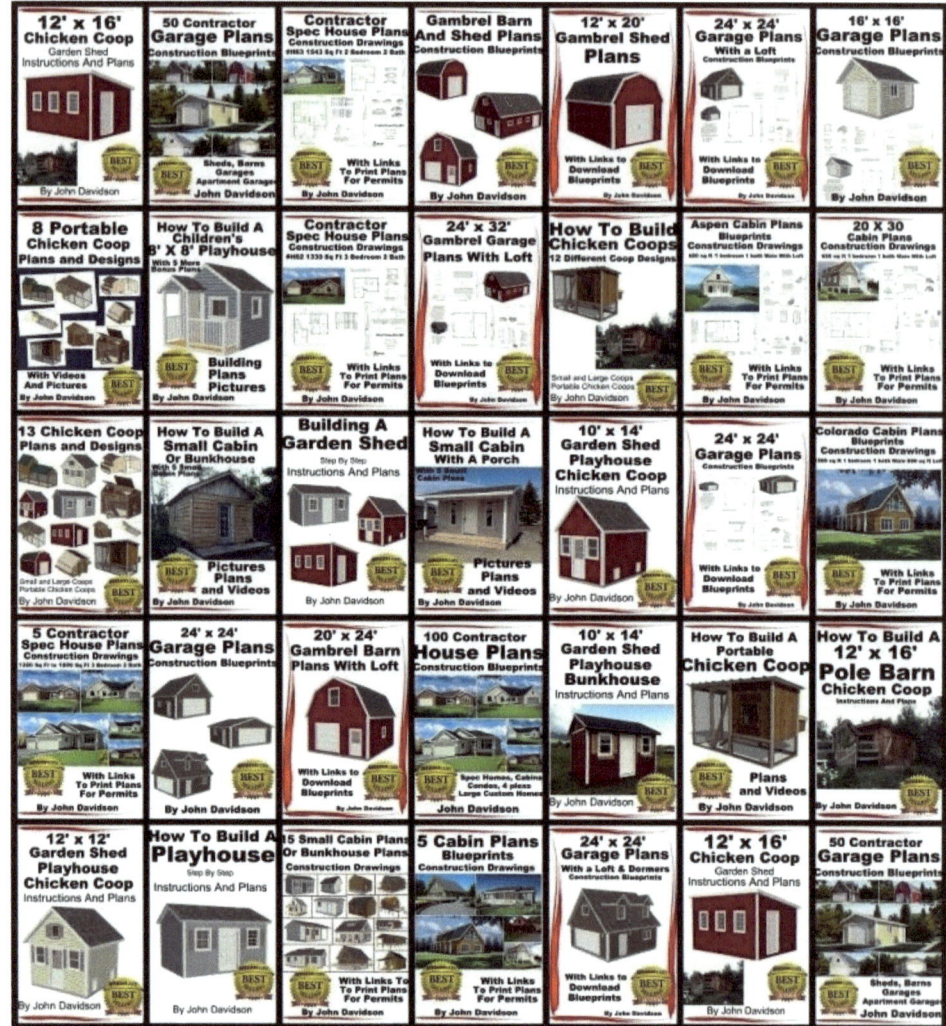

Entrepreneur Book Series

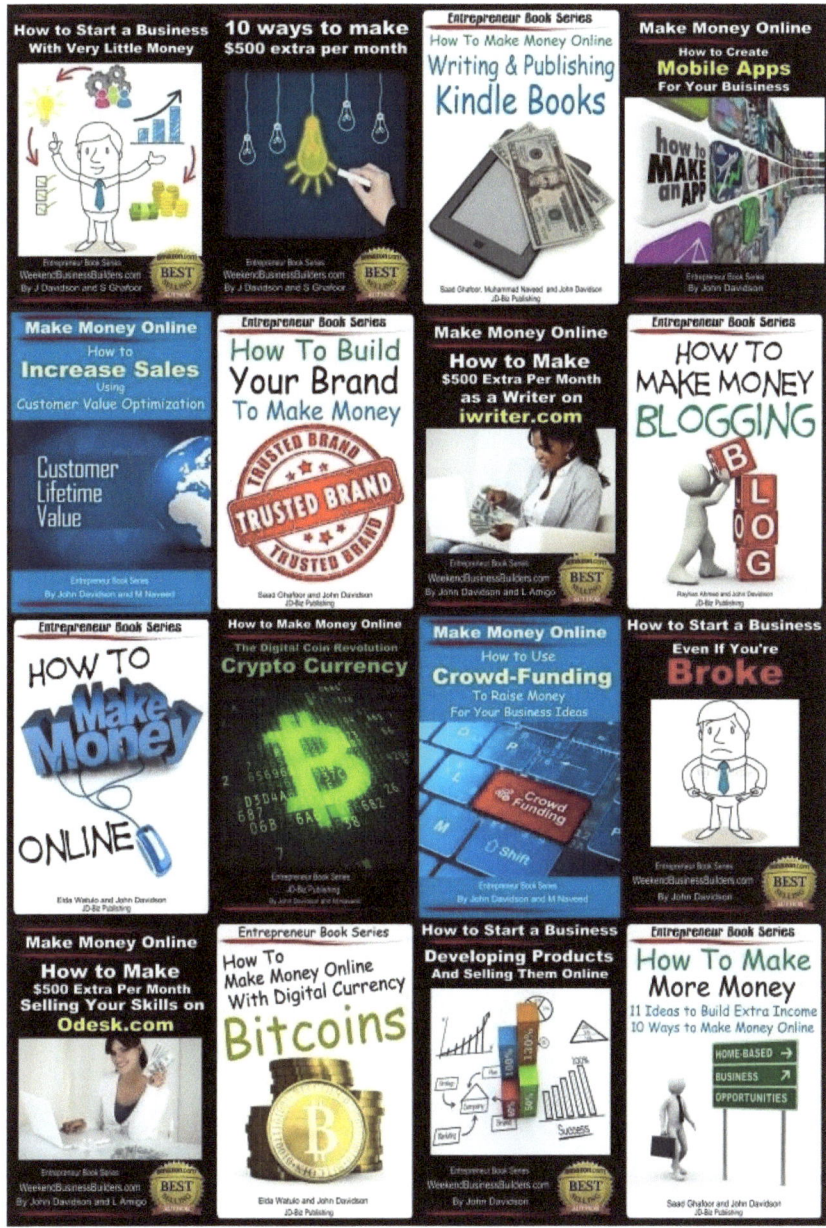

Our books are available at

1. Amazon.com

2. Barnes and Noble

3. Itunes

4. Kobo

5. Smashwords

6. Google Play Books

Download Free Books!

http://MendonCottageBooks.com

Publisher

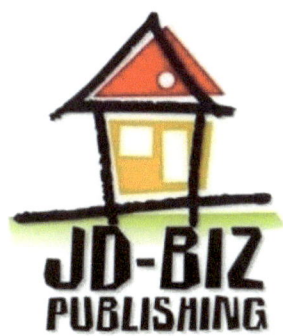

JD-Biz Corp

P O Box 374

Mendon, Utah 84325

http://www.jd-biz.com/

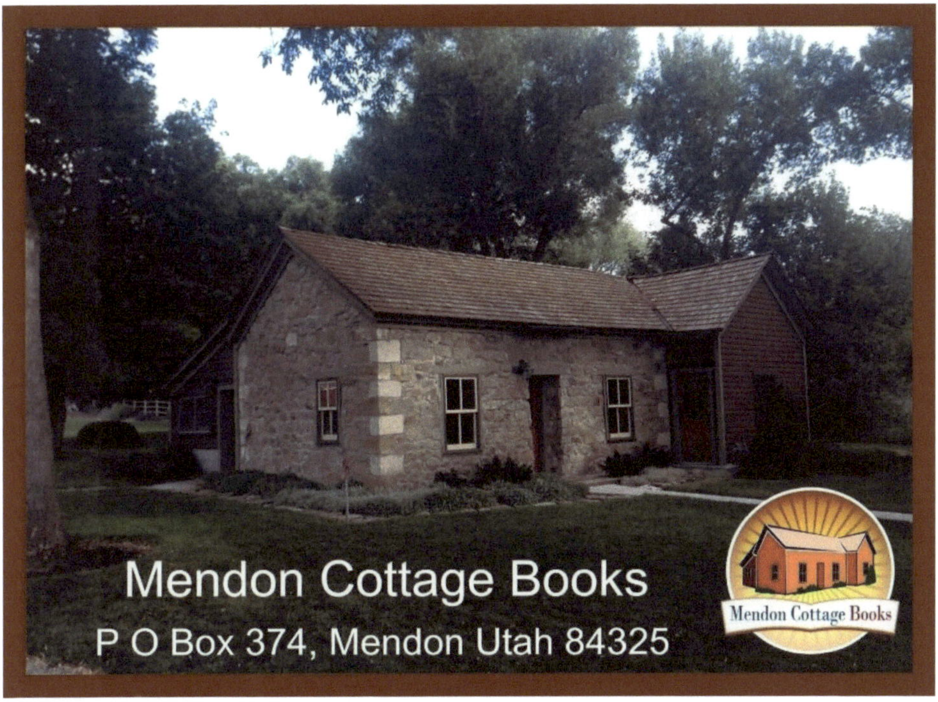

Mendon Cottage Books

P O Box 374, Mendon Utah 84325

Mendon Cottage Books

www.ingramcontent.com/pod-product-compliance
Lightning Source LLC
Chambersburg PA
CBHW040928180526
45159CB00002BA/658